52 Great Green Tomato Recipes

52 GREAT GREEN TOMATO RECIPES
by Phyllis Hobson

If you're like most of us, you reserve a fair amount of space in your garden for everyone's favorite crop—tomatoes. You make the most of their short summer season, eating them fresh and warm from the sun, slicing them for the table, canning them for next winter's casseroles. You know there's nothing better than vine-ripened tomatoes from your own garden.

And, like the rest of us, you dread that first fall frost because it means the end of the fresh tomato season. One of the most frost-tender of the garden plants, tomato vines may shrivel and die after even a light frost. An early September cold spell is especially frustrating because it may halt the ripening process or even kill the plant just when its crop is most abundant.

But you needn't lose the largest part of your tomato crop come fall. A frost needn't mean the end of fresh, red-ripe tomatoes for your dinner table. There are ways to ward off the damage of early, light frosts and even ways to thwart the late, hard frosts. And once they do take over, there are at least 50 ways to make delicious use of those green tomatoes you've picked from the vines.

First, though, you need to know when a frost is coming. During the last month of summer, the month before the usual first frost in your area, look for nature's first warning signals—a late afternoon nip in the air and a cloudless sky with no wind. If you aren't that attuned to weather signs, you can listen to your local weather reports. The evening radio or television news will warn you of any possibility of frost. If you are alerted by any of these warnings, head for the garden at sundown. A few minutes work now can save your tomatoes.

First, pick and refrigerate all the ripened tomatoes. If some are almost ripe, take them inside to ripen.

Now, cover the tomato vines with something lightweight for protection. You probably have something around the house—old bed sheets, light blankets, rolls of plastic sheeting, newspapers—almost anything that will keep the frost from the plants without breaking the vines. You needn't worry too much about tying them down. If there's enough wind to blow the coverings off, there's no danger of frost.

If it's late in the season, you may need to cover the plants each night for a while, until the weather warms up again. Be sure to uncover them each morning so they can benefit from the sun during the day.

If, in spite of your watchfulness, a light frost catches you unaware, don't give up. Very early the next morning, before the sun hits the frost-nipped tomato vines, get out the garden hose and spray the leaves thoroughly with cold water. If you act quickly enough and water them well enough, you may be able to prevent any damage from a light frost. Even if some damage is done by a heavier frost, you may be able to save some of the plants.

If fall weather is consistently cold and frosts are a nightly occurrence in your area, you may want to prolong the tomato season by constructing a mini-greenhouse right in your garden over the tomato vines. Such a greenhouse arrangement may be as elaborate as you want to make it, but a simple, yet inexpensive and very effective protection may be made with a few short posts, some used lumber and a roll of clear plastic sheeting.

To make it, drive the posts in the ground on each side close to the tomato vines. The top of the posts should just clear the top of the vines. Set the posts down the length of the garden four, six or eight feet apart, depending on the length of your used lumber. Then nail the boards from post to post to make a rough framework just wide enough and tall enough to cover the vines. Cover the framework with the plastic sheeting and fasten it with boards nailed on top of the framework.

Leave the plastic sheeting hanging loose down the sides. It may be weighted down with soil or stones on cold nights or raised for ventilation on warm days. It also may be raised at dinnertime to harvest the crop of tomatoes that will go right on ripening inside their warm, frost-free garden-row greenhouse.

No matter how you try to thwart him, though, if you live in almost any part of the northern hemisphere, you know Jack Frost is going to win eventually. He may come in September in the north or in November in the south, but sooner or later he's going to get your tomato vines.

But you don't have to let him have the tomatoes. If the weather has been warm, chances are that at least half of your crop, ranging from the dark green, marble-sized cherry tomatoes to the big, full-size, partly-pink Big Boys, still are on the vines at frost time. Every one of them can be a delicious, nutritious addition to your fall and winter meals if you know what to do with them.

First, let's take care of those that will ripen. Let's say winter is looming ahead in earnest now. You've successfully nursed your tomato vines through the first light frosts of fall, but now heavy frosts are forecast and the temperature may drop below freezing during the night. It's clear that the days of vine-ripened tomatoes are over. It's time to bring your tomatoes in from the garden.

That doesn't mean the days of red, ripe tomatoes are over. You can ripen them indoors and enjoy homegrown, ripe tomatoes for several weeks. It's true that they aren't quit as flavorful or as rich in Vitamin C as your summer tomatoes were, but they're a lot better—and a lot less expensive—than the supermarket variety.

As you look over your soon-to-be-frost-killed plants in the garden, first select those tomatoes that will be taken in to ripen indoors. The best candidates are the pink ones and larger, lighter-colored green tomatoes that have a whitish tint or glistening skins. As you go down the rows, pick off all the rest—the dark green ones—and set them inside in baskets or pans. They'll keep well at least a week in a cool place and you'll need them for the green tomato recipes we'll talk about later. For now, leave the larger, to-be-ripened tomatoes on the vines.

If you have an out-of-the-way basement or garage that you don't mind getting a little dirty, your work is almost over. You can simply pull up the tomato vines—complete with the lighter-colored tomatoes on them—and hang them upside down where the temperature is 55 to 65 degrees. Then all you have to do is pluck off the tomatoes as they ripen. Of course you'll have to clean up the dirt and tomato vine debris later.

A neater but just as satisfactory way to ripen green tomatoes over a period of six to eight weeks is to pick the larger tomatoes that have begun to ripen and spread them out on trays or shelves (but not on a dirt floor) in a cool, dark place, such as a fruit cellar. Use the tomatoes as they ripen. If you need a few extra for company, take them out a day or two ahead and place them on the windowsill to ripen in the sun.

If you don't have that much shelf space, wrap each tomato individually in a scrap of newspaper, then place the wrapped tomatoes, no more than two or three layers deep, in open crates or baskets. Store in a dark, cool place.

Or you may prefer this simpler, less-work version of the wrapping method. Just spread the tomatoes out one layer deep on a table and cover with newspapers or a cloth.

With all four methods, it's important to remember that ripe tomatoes are perishable. Check the ripening tomatoes every day (yes, even the newspaper-wrapped ones) and store any red ones in the refrigerator. A few will rot without ripening, but with careful tending and optimum storage temperatures, you could have fresh ripe tomatoes from your garden for Thanksgiving or even Christmas dinner.

With all the large tomatoes tucked away to ripen, it's time to turn your attention to those baskets of small tomatoes you set aside. It's possible to can, freeze or dry them for winter meals. They can be pickled and preserved in the old ways, just as your grandmother used them, or they can be used in main dishes, salads and desserts in some new ways that even grandmother never thought of. In addition, many of the main dishes and desserts may be made up and stored in the freezer for leaner days.

Green tomatoes also may be made to seem a lot more exotic than they are. With a little ingenuity, those discards from the garden can be converted into "olives" for relish trays, "figs" to be used in fillings for cakes and cookies, "apple" slices for pies and even a mock candied fruit for fruit cakes and puddings.

The following recipes will tell you how.

PRESERVING GREEN TOMATOES

Canned Slices

Wash, core and slice green tomatoes. Pack loosely in quart canning jars. Cover with boiling water to ½ inch of top of jars. Add ¼ teaspoon of salt to each jar if you wish. Process 20 minutes in boiling water bath.

To use, drain slices and prepare according to the recipes for green tomatoes as a vegetable, main dish or dessert.

Freezing Green Tomatoes

Wash and core green tomatoes without peeling. Cut in slices or cubes and spread in a single layer on a cookie sheet covered with waxed paper. Freeze, then remove from sheet and package frozen pieces in containers or plastic bags. Use in almost any of the following recipes for vegetables, main dishes, salads or desserts. Frozen slices may be dipped in flour and fried in hot oil without thawing. Salt and pepper to taste.

Dried Green Tomatoes

Peel and core green tomatoes and chop in cubes ½ inch or less in size. Drain. Line cookie sheets with waxed paper or aluminum foil and spread cubes one layer deep. Dry in commercial food drier or place outdoors in a well-ventilated, sunny location. Bring indoors at night to protect from dew. When perfectly dry, store in glass jars. Soak one hour in an equal amount of water before using in any recipe calling for chopped green tomatoes.

Green Tomato Butter

6 pounds (12 to 18 medium) green tomatoes
2 tablespoons powdered ginger
2 teaspoons powdered cinnamon
1 teaspoon powdered allspice
5 pounds brown sugar
Juice of two lemons
2 cups water

Coarsely chop green tomatoes without peeling or coring. Add remaining ingredients. Simmer over low heat two to three hours, until mixture is thick, stirring frequently. Run through colander or strainer to remove seeds and any hard bits of pulp. Reheat to boiling and pour into hot, sterilized pint canning jars. Seal immediately. Makes four pints.

Green Tomato Marmalade

24 medium green tomatoes
4 oranges
3½ pounds granulated sugar

Core and peel green tomatoes and cut in thin slices. Wash and peel oranges and cut peeling into thin strips. Cut oranges into thin slices. Combine tomato slices, peeling and orange slices with sugar in a kettle and let stand overnight. In the morning, place kettle over low heat and gradually bring mixture to a boil, stirring occasionally. Simmer gently about two hours, until thick. Pour immediately into hot, sterilized jelly jars and seal. Makes 6 pints.

Green Tomato Preserves

5 pounds green tomatoes
4 pounds granulated sugar
2 lemons, thinly sliced, with peeling

Core and peel tomatoes and chop fine. Add sugar and let set overnight. Drain liquid into a large kettle and boil rapidly until thickened. Add chopped green tomatoes and lemon slices. Cook until thick and clear. Pour, boiling hot, into hot, sterilized pint canning jars. Seal immediately. Makes 6 pints.

Preserving 7

Green Tomato Mincemeat

6 pounds (about 24 small) green tomatoes
10 to 12 small, tart apples
1 pound seedless raisins
4 cups brown sugar
½ cup vinegar
1 teaspoon salt
2 teaspoons powdered cinnamon
1 teaspoon ground nutmeg
1 teaspoon powdered cloves
½ teaspoon powdered ginger
1 orange
1 lemon

Core and quarter tomatoes and apples. Do not peel. Put both through coarse blade of food chopper. Combine with raisins, sugar, vinegar and spices in a large, open kettle and cook two hours over low heat, stirring frequently. Quarter the orange and lemon without peeling. Remove any seeds and run through fine blade of food chopper. Add to cooked mincemeat and stir well. To freeze, cool, then pack into pint containers. To can, fill pint jars to within ½ inch of top and process 30 minutes in boiling water bath. Recipe makes about 10 pints. One pint makes one mincemeat pie.

GREEN TOMATO PICKLES

Easy Green Tomato Dills

Wash small green cherry tomatoes but do not peel or core. Pack loosely in quart canning jars. To each jar add:

1 peeled garlic clove
½ teaspoon mixed pickling spices
1 sprig fresh dill
1 small piece hot red pepper (optional)

In a saucepan, combine:

2 quarts water
2 cups vinegar
1 cup flaked pickling salt

Bring to a boil and stir to dissolve salt. Pour over tomatoes in jars to within ¼ inch of tops. Seal jars at once. Let set six weeks to cure before eating. Keep refrigerated after opening.

Chow Chow

16 medium green tomatoes
1 medium head cabbage
6 medium onions
6 green peppers
6 sweet red peppers
¼ cup flaked pickling salt
2 tablespoons prepared mustard
6 cups vinegar
2½ cups sugar
1½ teaspoons turmeric
1 teaspoon powdered ginger
2 tablespoons mustard seeds
1 tablespoon celery seeds
1 tablespoon mixed whole pickling spices, tied in a cheesecloth bag

With a knife, coarsely chop all vegetables. Combine and mix with salt. Let stand overnight. Next morning drain, discarding liquid. Put prepared mustard in a large kettle and gradually blend in vinegar, sugar and spices. Simmer two minutes. Strain, then add chopped vegetables. Simmer another 10 minutes. Discard cheesecloth spice bag. Pack immediately into hot, sterilized jars to within ¼ inch of tops. Be sure liquid covers vegetables in jars. Seal at once. Process 10 minutes in boiling water bath. Use within six months. Makes 6 to 8 pints.

French Pickles

About 32 medium green tomatoes
3 large onions
½ cup flaked pickling salt
2 cups vinegar
3 cups brown sugar
½ cup white mustard seed
½ teaspoon powdered cloves
½ teaspoon powdered ginger
1 teaspoon dry mustard powder
¼ teaspoon cayenne pepper

Wash and core green tomatoes. Cut into ¼-inch slices. Peel onions and slice thinly. Combine, sprinkle with salt and mix well. Let set 12 hours, then drain well, discarding liquid. Add remaining ingredients and put into a large kettle. Bring to the simmering point over low heat and cook 15 minutes. Pack slices into pint canning jars and heat syrup to boiling point. Pour syrup over slices in jars to ¼ inch from top. Process 10 minutes in boiling water bath. Makes 6 pints.

Indian Pickles

8 medium green tomatoes, cored
8 medium ripe tomatoes, cored and peeled
3 medium onions, peeled
3 sweet red peppers, cored and seeded
1 large cucumber
7 cups celery, chopped
2/3 cup flaked pickling salt
6 cups vinegar
6 cups brown sugar
1 teaspoon dry mustard
1 teaspoon white pepper

Coarsely chop all vegetables. Sprinkle with salt and let stand overnight. In the morning, drain, discarding liquid. Combine with remaining ingredients in an open kettle. Place over low heat and bring to the simmering point slowly. Cook 30 minutes, stirring occasionally. Pack into hot, sterilized jars and seal at once. Process 10 minutes in boiling water bath. Makes 5 or 6 pints.

Sweet Pickle Slices

2 quarts sliced green tomatoes
3 tablespoons flaked pickling salt
2 cups vinegar
2/3 cup brown sugar
1 cup granulated sugar
3 tablespoons mustard seeds
1/2 teaspoon celery seeds
1 teaspoon powdered turmeric
3 cups thinly sliced onions
2 large sweet red peppers, chopped
1 hot green or red pepper, chopped (optional)

Combine tomato slices and salt. Let stand overnight, then drain, discarding liquid. In an open kettle, heat vinegar to boiling and add sugars and spices. Simmer 5 minutes then add onions and simmer another 5 minutes. Add drained tomato slices and peppers and return slowly to a boil. Simmer 5 minutes more, stirring occasionally with a wooden spoon. Pack, boiling hot, into hot, sterilized jars to 1/4 inch of tops, making sure syrup covers vegetables in each jar. Seal at once. Process 10 minutes in boiling water bath. Makes 4 to 6 pints.

Sweet Pickle Relish

1 gallon (about 32) green tomatoes
2 medium onions
4 green peppers
2 sweet red peppers
½ cup flaked pickling salt
1 teaspoon mixed pickling spices
1 tablespoon celery seed
3 (3-inch) cinnamon sticks
3 cups vinegar
1 cup water
2 cups sugar

Wash and core tomatoes. Peel onions. Core and seed peppers. Run all through coarse blade of food chopper. Mix in salt and let stand overnight. In the morning, drain well, discarding liquid. Tie mixed pickling spices in a cheesecloth bag and add to vegetables and remaining ingredients in an open kettle. Slowly bring to a simmer over low heat, stirring occasionally. Cook 30 minutes. Remove cinnamon sticks and cheesecloth bag and discard. Ladle relish into hot, sterilized jars and seal at once. Process 10 minutes in boiling water bath. Makes 12 pints.

Piccalilli

32 medium green tomatoes
1 large head cabbage
4 medium sweet red peppers
1 large onion
½ cup flaked pickling salt
1½ cups brown sugar
2 tablespoons mustard seed
1 tablespoon celery seed
1 tablespoon prepared horseradish
4½ cups vinegar

Wash and core tomatoes and cabbage. Core peppers and remove seeds. Peel onion. Run all through coarse blade of food chopper. Sprinkle with salt and mix well. Let set overnight and drain thoroughly in the morning, pressing to remove as much liquid as possible. Discard liquid. Meanwhile, add sugar, spices and horseradish to vinegar and bring to a boil. Simmer 15 minutes, then strain vinegar over vegetables and discard spices. Heat vegetables to boiling and pack into sterilized pint jars to within ½ inch of tops. Process 10 minutes in boiling water bath. Makes about 6 pints.

DISGUISING GREEN TOMATOES

Mock Apple Slices

16 small green tomatoes   ½ cup water
1 slice lemon   ½ ounce ginger root
¾ cup sugar   ¼ teaspoon salt

    Peel and core green tomatoes. Remove seedy centers and discard. Cut fleshy outer meat into strips and spread in a buttered baking dish. Combine remaining ingredients and pour over tomato strips. Cover and bake in a 350-degree oven 20 minutes. Uncover and bake 20 minutes longer. Remove ginger root. Serves 6. If desired, ½ teaspoon powdered cinnamon and ¼ teaspoon powdered ginger or two tablespoons red cinnamon candies may be substituted for the ginger root.

Green Tomato "Figs"

8 pounds small green tomatoes
8 pounds brown sugar

    Wash and core green tomatoes without peeling. Add sugar (but no water) and cook over very low heat until tomatoes are transparent, stirring carefully until sugar is melted. Remove tomatoes from syrup and spread in a single layer on a cookie sheet or drying rack, flattening each tomato with a fork. Add ½ teaspoon syrup to each "fig" and place in the sun to dry. Bring trays in at night, but return each morning to a sunny spot, adding ½ teaspoon syrup to each "fig" every two or three hours. When dry, the fruits will still be sticky, but will taste much like dried figs. Pack into tins or boxes, sprinkling each layer with powdered sugar. They may be frozen or will keep for several months in a cool place if well dried and protected from insects. Use as you would dried figs, in cookies, in cake fillings and puddings or eaten as a confection.

Candied Green Tomato Bits

4 medium green tomatoes
2 cups sugar
1 cup water

Wash green tomatoes and cut into quarters. Scoop out seeds and pulp and discard. Cut fleshy outer meat into small pieces and drain thoroughly. Combine sugar and water in a heavy skillet and bring to a boil over medium heat. Cook to the soft ball stage (238 degrees). Slowly add half the cut-up tomato pieces and simmer until clear. Remove pieces and drain. Reheat syrup to boiling and drop in remainder of green tomato pieces and repeat. When all pieces are cooked and drained, roll them in granulated sugar. Use in fruit cakes, candies, cookies or in any way you would use candied fruit. Will keep for several months in the refrigerator. May be frozen. If desired, syrup may be colored red or green or yellow with food coloring before adding tomato bits. A variety of colors is attractive in fruit cakes and cookies.

Green Tomato Olives

About 100 small, green cherry tomatoes
Several sprigs fresh dill
3 tablespoons mixed pickling spices
1½ cups flaked pickling salt
2 cups vinegar
8 quarts hot water

Wash and dry tomatoes. Do not core. Place a layer of dill and half the pickling spices in a stone crock or a largemouth, one-gallon glass jar. Top with all the tomatoes, then add another layer of dill and the remaining spices. In a saucepan, dissolve the salt in the vinegar and water and bring to a boil. Let cool, then pour over the tomatoes. Over the top place a small plate which has been weighted to keep all the tomatoes well covered by the brine. Any tomatoes not immersed will spoil and ruin the entire batch. Cover the jar with a cloth and keep in a cool place (60 to 70 degrees) about three weeks. Each day skim any scum off the top of the liquid, rinse off the plate and add more brine as necessary to keep tomatoes immersed. When tomatoes are well flavored and even in color, they are cured and ready to eat or can.

To can, drain the "olives" and prepare fresh hot brine by bringing ¾ cup salt, 1 cup vinegar and 4 quarts water to a boil, stirring to dissolve salt. Fill 12 pint or 6 quart canning jars with tomatoes and add a fresh sprig of dill, 1 peeled clove of garlic and 1 bay leaf to each jar. Pour hot brine in each jar to within ¼ inch of top. Process pints and quarts 10 minutes in boiling water bath. Serve as you would olives.

USING GREEN TOMATOES AS A VEGETABLE

Chilled Green Tomato Medley

¼ cup cooking oil
2 large or 3 medium green tomatoes, peeled and cut into 1-inch cubes
3 medium zucchini, unpeeled and cut into 1-inch cubes
¼ pound fresh mushrooms, sliced
¾ cup onions, chopped
½ cup celery, sliced
1 clove garlic, crushed
¼ cup red wine vinegar
1 tablespoon sugar
½ teaspoon salt
⅛ teaspoon pepper
1 cup ripe tomato cubes
¼ cup pimiento-stuffed olives, sliced

Heat oil in large skillet over medium heat and stir-fry green tomatoes, zucchini, mushrooms, onion, celery and garlic 10 minutes. Add vinegar, sugar, salt and pepper. Reduce heat to low and cover. Simmer 5 minutes more. Stir in ripe tomatoes and olives, increase heat until mixture comes to a boil, then turn off heat and spoon mixture into a large bowl. Refrigerate until well chilled. Serve cold. Makes 6 servings.

Stewed Green Tomatoes

3 medium onions
2 tablespoons cooking oil
6 large green tomatoes
½ cup water
2 tablespoons butter or margarine
1 tablespoon sugar
½ teaspoon salt

    Peel and thinly slice onions. Saute in cooking oil until transparent, but not browned. Meanwhile, peel and core green tomatoes and cut into ¼-inch slices. Add to skillet and saute, stirring gently two to three minutes. Add water, cover and simmer 10 minutes, until tomatoes are soft. Season to taste with butter or margarine, sugar and salt. Serves 6 to 8.

Green Tomatoes in Cream Sauce

4 large green tomatoes
1 egg yolk, beaten
½ cup fine, dry bread crumbs
6 tablespoons butter or margarine
2 tablespoons flour
1 cup milk
½ teaspoon salt
¼ cup grated Parmesan cheese

    Wash and core green tomatoes and cut into slices ½ inch thick. Dip in egg yolk, then in bread crumbs. Sauté in 4 tablespoons of the butter or margarine until golden brown. As slices are browned, arrange on a warm serving platter. When all slices are browned, add remaining butter or margarine to frying pan and blend in flour. Gradually stir in milk, add salt and cook over low heat until thickened, stirring constantly. Pour over tomato slices on serving platter. Sprinkle with Parmesan cheese. Serve hot. Serves 6 to 8.

Fried Green Tomatoes

1 medium green tomato per person
Flour
Salt and pepper
Cooking oil

    Wash, core and slice tomatoes in ⅓-inch slices. Do not peel. Dip each slice in flour, season to taste with salt and pepper and fry until golden in hot oil. Drain on paper toweling, then serve hot with butter or margarine.

Broiled Green Tomatoes

Select one large green tomato for each two servings. Wash and core tomatoes and cut in halves. For each half, dice ½ slice bacon. Arrange uncooked bacon bits on tomato halves and sprinkle with Parmesan cheese. Broil 10 minutes, or until bacon is crisp and tomato top is lightly browned.

USING GREEN TOMATOES IN MAIN DISHES

Baked Green Tomatoes

6 large green tomatoes
  Salt
8 eggs
½ teaspoon salt
¼ teaspoon dried basil
2 tablespoons cooking oil

1 cup shredded cheddar cheese
1 cup bread cubes
¼ cup grated Parmesan cheese

Cut tops off green tomatoes. Remove centers with a spoon, reserving enough pulp to make one cup. Discard remaining pulp. Salt insides of shells and set upside down to drain. Beat eggs slightly with a fork. Add ½ teaspoon salt and basil. Heat oil in large skillet. Lower heat and add beaten eggs. Cook, stirring frequently, until eggs are set, but still slightly moist. Combine with cheese, bread cubes and one cup reserved tomato pulp. Spoon into tomato shells and place shells in shallow baking dish. Top with Parmesan cheese and bake 15 minutes in 350-degree oven. Serves 8.

Green tomato shells also may be filled with any of the following:

Macaroni and cheese
Cooked succotash (half lima beans and half corn)
Bread stuffing with cooked, chopped meat or mushrooms
Spanish rice

Bake 20 minutes in a 350-degree oven and serve hot.

Green Tomato Croquettes

2 cups canned or fresh tomatoes, chopped and drained
Cracker crumbs, finely rolled
Salt and pepper to taste
Hot oil for frying

To the chopped tomatoes add enough cracker crumbs to make a mixture easy to handle. Shape into 1½-inch balls or cylinders four inches long. Roll in cracker crumbs or flour and fry in hot cooking oil at least two inches deep. Serve as a meat substitute or accompaniment. Serves 6.

Spinach Loaf

2 eggs, well beaten
1 cup cooked spinach, chopped
2½ cups green tomatoes, chopped and drained
1 cup cheddar cheese, shredded
1 cup soft bread crumbs
Salt and pepper
3 slices bacon, diced
1 tablespoon minced onion
1 tablespoon green pepper, chopped
2 tablespoons flour

Combine eggs, spinach, 1 cup green tomatoes, cheese and bread crumbs. Season to taste with salt and pepper and put in a greased loaf pan. Bake in 350-degree oven 30 minutes. Serve hot with sauce made by frying diced bacon until crisp. Sauté onion and green pepper in bacon fat. Add remaining 1½ cups chopped green tomatoes and stir fry 3 to 5 minutes, until tomato is cooked. Stir in flour and cook until thickened. Season to taste and pour over loaf. Serves 6.

Cheese Loaf

2 cups canned or fresh green tomatoes, chopped and drained
1 egg
Day-old bread crumbs
1 cup cheddar cheese, grated
Salt and pepper to taste
1 tablespoon onion, finely chopped
½ cup catsup

Combine green tomatoes and egg. Add as much bread crumbs as the mixture will absorb. Add cheese, seasoning and onion and shape into a loaf. Bake in 350-degree oven 30 to 40 minutes, until the loaf is firm and beginning to brown. Decorate top with catsup and return to oven 5 minutes more. Serve as a main course. Serves 4 to 6.

Tasty Stacks

4 medium green tomatoes
1 egg, beaten
½ cup flour
½ teaspoon salt
6 tablespoons cooking oil
Processed cheese slices
4 tablespoons onion, minced
1 cup tomato sauce
1 teaspoon sugar
½ teaspoon salt

Core tomatoes and cut into ¼-inch slices. Dip each slice in the beaten egg, then in the flour to which the salt has been added. Sauté slices in hot oil, turning to brown on both sides. Arrange slices in a shallow baking dish in stacks, with slices of cheese between the tomato slices and on top of each stack. Sauté onion in skillet, then add tomato sauce, sugar and salt. Heat to boiling. Pour over green tomato stacks and bake in 350-degree oven 30 minutes, until cheese is melted and lightly browned on top. Each stack is a serving. Serves 4 to 6.

Baked Green Tomatoes with Eggs

4 green tomatoes, sliced
6 hard-cooked eggs
2 tablespoons green pepper, chopped
4 tablespoons butter or margarine
4 tablespoons flour
2 cups milk
Salt and pepper to taste
½ cup buttered bread or cracker crumbs

Spread tomato slices over bottom of a 1½-quart casserole. Shell and chop hard-cooked eggs and set aside. Sauté green pepper in butter or margarine. Stir in flour and gradually add milk. Cook over low heat, stirring constantly, until thickened. Season to taste with salt and pepper. Add chopped eggs and pour over tomato slices. Top with buttered crumbs and bake 30 minutes in 350-degree oven. Serves 6.

Green Tomato Omelet

1 tablespoon onion, minced
¼ cup green tomato, chopped fine
2 tablespoons butter or margarine, melted

2 eggs, well beaten
Salt and pepper

Sauté onion and green tomato in melted butter or margarine in a small skillet over low heat until onion is transparent and green tomato pieces are lightly browned. Spread evenly over bottom of pan and pour beaten eggs over all. Season to taste with salt and pepper. Cook over low heat. As egg begins to firm, lift edges and tilt pan to allow liquid to run underneath. Cook until bottom is golden brown and top is set but still moist. Fold over and serve hot. Makes one omelet. Increase ingredients in proportion for larger omelets or make one or more omelets per person.

Scalloped Egg—Green Tomato Casserole

6 hard-cooked eggs, peeled and sliced
1½ cups cubed green tomatoes, drained
5 tablespoons butter or margarine

¾ cup soft bread crumbs
3 tablespoons flour
1½ cups milk
½ teaspoon salt

Cover bottom of a casserole dish with half of egg slices. Top with half of green tomato cubes. Repeat. In a saucepan, melt 2 tablespoons butter or margarine and add bread crumbs. Stir well, then empty onto piece of waxed paper and set aside. Melt remaining butter or margarine in saucepan and stir in flour. Gradually add milk and salt and cook over low heat, stirring constantly, until thick. Pour sauce over eggs and green tomatoes in casserole and top with buttered bread crumbs. Bake in 350-degree oven 30 to 45 minutes. Serves 4 to 6.

Spanish Casserole

- 1 pound ground beef
- 1 small onion, minced
- 1 tablespoon green pepper, chopped
- 1 tablespoon sweet red pepper, chopped
- 1½ pounds firm green tomatoes, thickly sliced (about 5 cups)
- ½ teaspoon salt
- ¼ teaspoon garlic salt
- ¼ teaspoon ground cumin seed
- Dash of cayenne
- 1 cup tomato sauce
- 1½ cups canned or frozen whole kernel corn, cooked

Saute beef, onion and green and red peppers in medium skillet. Add remaining ingredients and mix well. Pour into oiled casserole. Bake 30 to 45 minutes in 350-degree oven. Serves 6.

Busy Day Casserole

- 1 pound ground beef
- 1 small onion, chopped
- ½ green pepper, chopped
- 1 clove garlic, minced
- 1 teaspoon salt
- 2 cups tomato sauce
- 4 medium green tomatoes, sliced
- 1 cup cheddar cheese, shredded

Sauté ground beef, onion, green pepper and garlic until meat loses its red color. Add salt and tomato sauce and cook over low heat 15 to 20 minutes, until thickened. Spread one-half of the green tomato slices in the bottom of a greased casserole dish, top with one-half the cheese, then with one-half the ground beef mixture. Repeat layers. Bake 30 minutes in 350-degree oven. Serves 6.

Leftover Loaf

2 cups leftover roast beef
   or lamb, chopped
2 cups leftover cooked
   pork or chicken, chopped
1½ cups green tomatoes, cut
   into ½-inch cubes,
   drained

1 cup soft bread crumbs
½ small onion, minced
1 tablespoon celery,
   chopped
½ teaspoon dried sage,
   crushed
Salt and pepper to taste

Combine all ingredients. Form into a loaf and bake 45 minutes in a 350-degree oven. Serves 6.

Meat Pie

1 cup fine, dry bread
   crumbs
2 cups leftover roast beef,
   cubed
3 medium green tomatoes,
   sliced

4 tablespoons butter or
   margarine
Salt and pepper
¼ cup Parmesan cheese

In a casserole dish arrange ½ cup bread crumbs, 1 cup beef cubes, half the green tomato slices and 2 tablespoons butter or margarine, cut into bits. Repeat layers, seasoning each layer to taste with salt and pepper. Top with Parmesan cheese and bake 20 to 40 minutes in a 350-degree oven. Serves 6.

Green Tomato Parmigiana

4 large or 6 medium green
   tomatoes
1 egg, well beaten
½ cup flour
½ teaspoon salt
   Hot oil for frying (about ¼
   cup)
2 cups tomato sauce

¼ teaspoon dried oregano
½ teaspoon salt
1 teaspoon sugar
½ cup grated Parmesan
   cheese
8 ounces mozzarella cheese,
   shredded

Core green tomatoes without peeling and cut into slices. Dip each slice into the beaten egg, then into the flour which has been mixed with ½ teaspoon salt. Fry in hot oil until

Main Dishes   21

golden, turning to brown both sides. Drain on paper towels until all slices are fried. Arrange one-half the slices in a shallow baking dish. In a bowl or saucepan, combine tomato sauce with oregano, remaining ½ teaspoon salt and sugar. Pour one-half the sauce over the green tomato slices. Sprinkle with one-half the Parmesan cheese, then one-half the mozzarella cheese. Repeat. Bake in 350-degree oven 25 to 30 minutes, until bubbly hot and golden brown. Serves 6.

Tamale Pie

1 teaspoon salt
2½ cups boiling water
1 cup yellow cornmeal
½ cup cold water
2 tablespoons cooking oil
1 pound ground beef
1 medium onion, chopped
½ green pepper, chopped
1 cup green tomatoes, chopped and drained

2 mild chili peppers, chopped
1 cup ripe tomatoes, fresh or canned
1 teaspoon ground cumin seed
Chili powder to taste
Salt and pepper to taste

Add salt to boiling water. Slowly add cornmeal which has been mixed with cold water. Cook 15 minutes over low heat, stirring frequently. Meanwhile, sauté ground beef, onion and green pepper in skillet until meat loses its red color. Add green tomato cubes and chili peppers and fry, stirring frequently, until lightly browned. Add ripe tomatoes, cumin, chili powder, salt and pepper. Simmer 10 minutes. Alternate layers of cooked cornmeal and meat mixture in a well-greased casserole. Bake 30 minutes in a 350-degree oven. Serves 4 to 6.

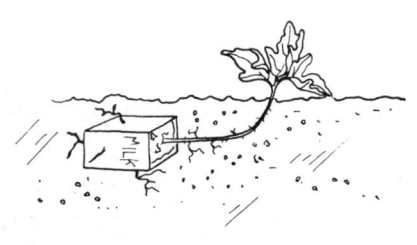

USING GREEN TOMATOES IN SALADS AND SALAD DRESSINGS

Tossed Salad

2 tablespoons tarragon or wine vinegar
½ teaspoon salt
1 clove garlic, crushed
Freshly ground pepper
2 pounds assorted greens (head lettuce, Romaine, bibb, endive or leaf lettuce), washed and chilled
½ pound fresh spinach, washed and chilled, ribs removed
¼ cup salad oil
3 medium green tomatoes, peeled and cut into small cubes
1 cup sliced radishes
3 green onions, finely sliced
¼ cup crumbled bleu cheese

About two hours before serving, combine vinegar, salt, garlic and pepper in a bottle or jar. Shake well and let stand at room temperature. At serving time, tear lettuce and spinach leaves in bite-size pieces into a large salad bowl. Pour oil over all and toss until leaves are evenly coated. Add green tomatoes, radishes, onions and cheese. To serve, strain vinegar onto salad and toss well. Serves 6 to 8.

Carrot Salad

1 cup shredded raw carrots
2 medium green tomatoes, peeled, diced and drained
1 cup diced celery
Lettuce
French dressing
Garlic salt

Combine carrots, green tomatoes and celery. Arrange on servings of lettuce and top with French dressing seasoned with garlic salt.

Cabbage-Apple Salad

1 large head cabbage
1 cup celery, diced
2 cups red apples, cored and diced, but not peeled
1 green pepper, diced
½ cup walnuts or pecans, chopped
2 medium green tomatoes, chopped
½ cup sweet Russian dressing
Unpeeled red apple slices

Remove coarse outer leaves from cabbage. Cut an even slice off the top, then invert cabbage and remove the core in one piece. Using a sharp knife, remove most of the inner portion of the cabbage from the cored end, leaving a solid shell which will stand upright. Trim top evenly. From the inner portion, prepare 2 cups shredded cabbage. Reserve remainder for other dishes. Combine shredded cabbage with celery, apple, green pepper, nuts and green tomato. Add dressing and toss lightly with two forks. Pile lightly into the cabbage shell. Serve on a lettuce-lined platter garnished with unpeeled apple slices. Serves 6 to 8.

Fruit Salad

1 orange
2 medium green tomatoes, chopped and drained
2 teaspoons sugar
3 fresh peaches or 6 canned peach halves, chopped and drained
¼ cup finely diced celery
¼ cup finely diced apple
Mayonnaise or salad dressing
Lettuce leaves
6 fresh Bing cherries or canned Maraschino cherries

Peel orange and chop pulp. Add to chopped green tomato and sugar. Let set while peeling and chopping other fruits and celery. When all are prepared, combine orange-green tomato mixture with peaches, celery and apple. Moisten with mayonnaise or salad dressing. Serve on lettuce leaves garnished with cherries. Serves 6.

SALAD DRESSINGS

Thousand Island Dressing

2 medium green tomatoes
1 cup mayonnaise or salad dressing
1 tablespoon green pepper, chopped
1 tablespoon sweet red pepper, chopped
¼ teaspoon paprika
2 tablespoons chopped olives

Peel green tomatoes and scoop seeds and pulp from centers. Discard pulp and finely chop outer shells. Combine with remaining ingredients and mix well. Makes about two cups dressing. Will keep a week or two in the refrigerator.

Creamy French Dressing

2 medium green tomatoes
4 tablespoons lemon juice or vinegar
4 tablespoons catsup
¼ teaspoon paprika
¼ teaspoon salt
⅛ teaspoon garlic salt
1 tablespoon honey
Few grains cayenne pepper
½ cup salad oil

Peel green tomato. Scoop out and discard seeds and pulp. Cut shell in pieces and put in blender. Add lemon juice, catsup, paprika, salt, garlic salt, honey and cayenne. Blend until smooth. Gradually add oil, one teaspoon at a time, with blender running on low speed. Makes about two cups dressing. Will keep well in refrigerator.

Cooked Salad Dressing or Sandwich Spread

- 8 medium green tomatoes
- 4 sweet red peppers
- 4 medium onions
- 3 cucumbers
- ½ cup flaked pickling salt
- 2 teaspoons celery seed
- 1 teaspoon powdered mustard
- ¼ teaspoon black pepper
- 1 cup sugar
- 2½ cups vinegar
- 1 teaspoon mixed pickling spices
- 2 eggs
- ½ cup flour
- ¾ cup salad oil

Wash and core green tomatoes and peppers. Peel onion. Wash cucumbers but leave unpeeled. Run all four vegetables through coarse blade of food chopper. Sprinkle with salt, cover and let stand 12 hours or overnight. Next day, drain well and place in a kettle. Add celery seed, mustard, pepper, sugar and 2¼ cups vinegar (reserve ¼ cup). Tie pickling spices in a small piece of cheesecloth and add. Bring slowly to the simmering point and cook over low heat 30 minutes. Meanwhile, in a two-quart bowl or blender jar, combine eggs and flour with reserved ¼ cup vinegar. Using an egg beater, electric mixer or blender, beat mixture until thick, then add oil in a very thin, steady stream as you continue beating until smooth. Add to the mixed vegetables, remove the pickling spice bag and cook until thick, stirring frequently. Pour in four, sterile, pint-size canning jars and seal for five minutes in a boiling water bath. Will keep in the refrigerator for several weeks.

USING GREEN TOMATOES IN DESSERTS

Cake with Green Tomato Filling

1 cup sugar	3 cups cake flour
1/3 cup butter or margarine	1/2 teaspoon salt
2 eggs, slightly beaten	3 teaspoons baking powder
1 cup water	1 teaspoon vanilla

Cream sugar and butter or margarine until fluffy. Add eggs and water and blend well. In a separate bowl, combine cake flour, salt and baking powder. Gradually add, one-half cup at a time, to batter, blending well after each addition. Beat in vanilla. Divide batter among three 8- or 9-inch layer cake pans which have been greased, then dusted with flour. Bake in a 350-degree oven 25 to 30 minutes, until lightly browned and a touch of a finger will not leave an impression. While cake cools, combine in a large saucepan:

3 green tomatoes, peeled and chopped	1/2 teaspoon ground nutmeg
1 1/2 cups brown sugar	2 tablespoons butter or margarine
1 teaspoon powdered cinnamon	

Bring to a boil over low heat and simmer until thick, stirring constantly. Chill.

When cake layers and filling have cooled, assemble cake, spreading one-third of the filling between each layer and on top. Serves 10 to 12.

Old-Fashioned Filled Cookies

COOKIE BATTER:
1½ cups sugar
½ cup butter or margarine
1 egg, well beaten
½ cup milk
3½ cups flour
2 teaspoons baking soda
2 teaspoons cream of tartar
½ teaspoon salt

    Cream sugar and butter or margarine until fluffy. Add egg and milk and blend well. In a small bowl combine flour, soda, cream of tartar and salt. Add to creamed mixture and blend well. Chill at least one hour.

FILLING:
½ cup sugar
1 tablespoon cornstarch
1½ cups canned or fresh green tomatoes, chopped and drained
Grated rind and juice of 1 lemon

    In a saucepan, combine sugar, cornstarch and tomato pieces. Cook over low heat, stirring constantly, until very thick. Add grated rind and juice of lemon, stir well and heat again to bubbling. Chill.
    To assemble cookies, roll chilled dough to ⅛-inch thickness and cut cookies with the outer ring of a doughnut cutter or cookie cutter. Top half the cookies with 1 tablespoon chilled filling. Using the center ring of doughnut cutter or a thimble, cut the center from the remaining half of the cut-out cookies and place on top of filled halves. Crimp edges with a fork to seal and bake in a 350-degree oven 15 to 20 minutes, until lightly browned. Makes 3 to 4 dozen cookies, depending on size.

Green Tomato Pie

Pastry for two-crust pie
2 cups green tomatoes, cut in ½-inch cubes
Pinch of salt
1 tablespoon flour
1 cup sugar
1 tablespoon lemon juice
1 tablespoon butter or margarine
1 teaspoon powdered cinnamon
¼ teaspoon ground nutmeg

Line a 9-inch pie pan with one-half the pastry. Roll out remainder for top and cut four 1-inch slits in the center. Combine remaining ingredients and fill pie shell. Top with rolled-out pastry and crimp edges to seal. Bake 45 minutes in 350-degree oven. Serves 6.

Oatmeal Crumble

3 cups canned or fresh green tomatoes, chopped and drained (reserve ¼ cup juice)
½ cup brown sugar
¼ teaspoon powdered cinnamon
1 tablespoon butter or margarine
¼ cup reserved juice
⅔ cup flour
⅛ teaspoon salt
¼ teaspoon baking soda
⅔ cup uncooked rolled oats
⅓ cup sugar
¼ cup butter, margarine or vegetable shortening, melted

Spread chopped green tomatoes in the bottom of a greased shallow baking pan. Sprinkle with brown sugar and cinnamon which have been mixed. Dot with 1 tablespoon butter or margarine cut into pieces. Pour juice over top. In a mixing bowl, combine flour, salt, soda, oats and sugar. Stir in melted shortening to make a crumbly mixture. Spread evenly over the green tomato mixture. Bake in a 350-degree oven until lightly browned. Serve warm plain or with cream. Serves 6.

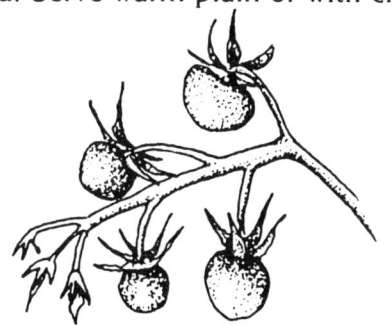

Drop Cookies

¾ cup sugar
½ cup vegetable shortening
½ cup honey
2 eggs, well beaten
2 tablespoons milk
2¾ cups flour
1 cup dried green tomato "figs" (page 12)
3 tablespoons candied green tomato bits (page 13)
½ cup shredded coconut
½ cup walnuts, chopped
3 teaspoons baking powder
½ teaspoon salt
1 teaspoon lemon extract

Cream sugar and shortening until fluffy. Add honey, eggs and milk. Stir ¾ cup flour into the chopped "figs," candied green tomato bits, coconut and chopped nuts. Set aside. Combine remaining 2 cups flour, baking powder and salt and add to creamed mixture. Fold in fruit-nut mixture and lemon extract. Drop by teaspoonfuls onto well-greased cookie sheets. Bake 12 to 15 minutes in 350-degree oven. Makes three dozen cookies.

Green Tomato Spice Cake

2 cups green tomatoes, chopped
1½ cups sugar
½ cup vegetable shortening
2 eggs, beaten
2 teaspoons baking soda
1 teaspoon salt
1 teaspoon powdered cinnamon
½ teaspoon ground nutmeg
½ teaspoon powdered cloves
2 cups flour
½ cup seedless raisins
½ cup walnuts, chopped

Simmer chopped green tomatoes and ½ cup sugar until tomatoes are well cooked and transparent. Strain through a colander or sieve to remove seeds, cores and skins. There should be 1¼ cups pulp. Cool. Cream remaining 1 cup sugar and shortening until fluffy. Add the eggs. Blend soda into cooled tomato pulp and add gradually to creamed mixture, beating well after each addition. In a separate bowl, combine salt, spices and flour. Gradually add all but one cup of the flour mixture to the batter, beating well. Finally, add raisins and nuts to remaining 1 cup flour and mix to coat well. Add, all at once, to batter and beat well. Pour into a well-greased and floured square cake pan and bake in 350-degree oven 35 to 40 minutes, until lightly browned and the touch of a finger does not leave an impression. Serve plain or frosted.

Green Tomato Bread

8 to 10 medium green tomatoes
⅔ cup seedless raisins
⅔ cup boiling water
⅔ cup vegetable shortening
2⅔ cups sugar
4 eggs
3⅓ cups flour
2 teaspoons baking soda
1½ teaspoons salt
½ teaspoon baking powder
1 teaspoon powdered cinnamon
1 teaspoon powdered cloves
⅔ cup pecans, or walnuts, coarsely chopped

Peel and core green tomatoes. Discard seeds. Run cut-up pieces through blender until smooth and creamy. You should have 2 cups pulp. Set raisins to soak in ⅔ cup boiling water and set aside to cool. In a large mixing bowl, cream shortening and sugar until fluffy. Add eggs, 2 cups tomato pulp and the plumped raisins and water in which they were soaked. Beat well. In another bowl, combine flour, soda, salt, baking powder, cinnamon, cloves and nuts. Add, one cup at a time, to mixture in large bowl, stirring well after each addition. Divide batter into two 9 × 5-inch greased loaf pans and bake in 350-degree oven 1 hour, 10 minutes, or until toothpick inserted in center comes out clean.